Praise for *Are You Cute?*

"Pat Noble has written an excellent book for women and teenage girls who wish to see themselves as God sees them. Drawing from her own life experience as a parent and church youth worker, Pat has given us a powerful tool to enable women of all ages to experience their true identity, and discover how "CUTE" their Maker really has created them to be."

Dr. Tony Evans
Senior Pastor, Oak Cliff Bible Fellowship
President, The Urban Alternative

ARE YOU

PAT NOBLE

Are You Cute?
by Pat Noble

Printed in the United States of America

ISBN 978-1-60791-719-9

www.xulonpress.com

From one CUTE Jesus
lady to another!

much love,

Pat
"2021"

DEDICATION

This book is lovingly dedicated
to my husband, Tony,
who heard my vision and said "Go do it."
Thank you for putting up with my "cuteness"
for the past thirty-two years.
I have loved you since the day the Lord
brought us together
and I will always love you until the end.

To my earthly father and mother,
Charles and Sarah Jackson,
who gave me the greatest gift of all
during my childhood,
the knowledge of our Lord and Savior.
Thank you for leading me to Christ
and being examples of Godly parents.
I love you Daddy and Mama.

To my daughter, Shawn,
who is with the Lord.
Though your time was very short on earth,
it was through you that I developed a personal
relationship with Jesus Christ and learned
to truly depend upon His Word.
I will see you again one day.
You are forever in my heart.

CONTENTS

ACKNOWLEGEMENTS

This book or ministry would not exist if I did not respond to the tug of the Holy Spirit. I want to thank my Lord and Savior, Jesus Christ for the vision and for not letting me rest until His purpose was accomplished. I want to thank Him for all the people He sent my way to make this a reality. I pray that God will richly bless each one of them for being a blessing to me. I want to thank Him for always proving to me that I am truly Covered Until The End.

To my **CUTE TEAM**, Tony Noble, Reggie Dukes, Joanne Dukes, Ryan Noble, Branden Noble, Danielle Noble: Words cannot express my gratitude and thanks for all you have done to make this vision a reality. You each felt it not robbery to freely give of your time and talents. Your enthusiasm and encouragement have been priceless. I know the Lord sent you and you have been invaluable. God bless you all for sowing into this ministry. No team could have done better!

- Reggie: Thank you for being patient with me and holding my hand while lending your expertise. You will never know how much I appreciate you taking the time to educate me and making sure that I understand different aspects of the venture. You are a master at what you do.
- Joanne: Thank you for encouraging me to write down all of my thoughts which resulted in this book. Thank you for praying with me and for me during some rough moments. I am blessed to have you as a friend and sister in Christ.
- Tony, Ryan, Danielle, Branden: What can you say to your family who pretty much has to help you? Thank you for cheering me on and pushing me forward when I thought of giving up. Thank you for ignoring my highs and lows and loving me in spite of them. Ryan, your enthusiasm and technical expertise with the website is invaluable. Danielle, thank you for your insights and suggestions for fashion items. Thank you also for giving me an illustration to use in my writing. I feel blessed that you are a part of this family and I look forward to having female reinforcement. Branden, your help with computer related issues while I was writing this book saved me valuable time. You all are the loves of my life.

To my Pastor, Tony Evans: You have not only been my pastor for the past fourteen years, but you have also been a big brother and a friend. Thank you for always preaching the Word and living it. Thank you for helping me through some of the hardest trials I have had to face. Your challenge to us to share the gospel helped to spark the CUTE concept. Your encouragement and love will always be remembered. You have been a strong tower in my life. I pray that God will continue to use you with the wonderful gift of preaching the Word.

To my sister, accountability partner, and friend, Sylvia Stewart: Words cannot express my gratitude and love for you and our friendship. Even though we have only known each other for thirteen years, our bond is for life. Circumstances brought us together, but the love of the Lord has kept us together. You have been instrumental to my growth and walk in Christ and I will forever be grateful to you. One of the gifts you gave me in 2001 for my birthday was a travel bible. Whenever I opened it up to study, I would always first read the inscription you wrote. Now it is for you. *"To my sister Sylvia, we met thirteen years ago sharing the Word and will share it forever because of our common denominator Jesus Christ. So please accept this "Word" as a lasting bond between two sisters."* I love you dearly.

To my village sisters: Anne Haynes, Shirley Griffin, Evelyn Brown, Derolyn Haley, Sandra Carter, Linda-Mitchell Hill, Debra Lowe, Nina Gines, Ruth Burton, Judy Jennings, Loretta Adams, Georgette Spain, Loretta Honore, Valerie Giglio and Belinda

Lawson: Thank you for your help and encouragement through the years as we all banded together to raise our children and deal with family issues. I could not have done it without you stepping in just in time and lending a helping hand or giving me Godly advice. You each are very dear to me and I deeply cherish our friendships.

To my drama sister and brother, Pat Jones and Pastor Rodney Carter: Thank you for your guidance and encouragement with the drama ministry. You have allowed me the freedom to utilize the gift God has given me and to stretch the limits to strive for uniqueness and excellence. Pat, I remember the glow, the smile on your face, and the excitement you had when I shared the CUTE concept with you. You grabbed my hand and instantly prayed for the ministry and its success. Thank you for giving me the push I needed to keep going.

To Jocelyn Wrighting, Carolyn Leake, Felecia Trimble, and Opera Brown: Little did you know that the discussion in the restroom at church while comforting Jocelyn resulted in the spark that propelled me to begin this ministry. Thank you for embracing the CUTE concept when I explained its meaning.

To my lifetime sisters, Gale Artemus, Avis Buchanan, and Rosilyn Outen: We have known each other since childhood and you all have stood by me and encouraged me in all my endeavors. I look forward to our lunches and girl talks whenever I go home to South Carolina. Even though distance separates us physically, we are forever linked spiritually.

Thank you for being the best friends a sister can have and for always being there.

To Carole Whitfield Shannon: Thank you for allowing me to be a friend and mentor to you throughout the years. Little did you know that while trying to encourage you in seeking your purpose in life, God was using you to encourage me. I know that your book will help others to claim their spiritual identity. I encourage you to continue to write for the Lord.

To my father and mother-in-law, John and Saiko Richmond, my brother-in-law, Van (who has gone home to be with the Lord), his wife, Michiko, and my other sister-in-law, Kimiko: Thank you for loving me as a daughter and sister. I have been blessed to have you all in my life.

To my blood sisters and brother, Charlesena Jackson, Debbie Smith, and Charles P. Jackson: Thank you for loving me in spite of me. Through all the ups and downs of life, we have stayed together. Thank you for your prayers and encouragement of this ministry.

To my nieces, Tia Finley, Rieako Johnson, Chewanne Smith, and Erika Johnson: Thank you for loving your crazy Aunt Pat. You are crown jewels in the Lord's eyes. I pray that you will always live like God's masterpieces. Thank you, Chewanne, for helping me get started on the initial design of the logo.

To my great niece, Madison Finley: Madison, thank you for telling me how cute I am and being an example for me to use. One day you will fully understand it all. You are precious and Aunt Pat loves you dearly.

Thank you Matthew Anderson: When I said I wanted "Wow", you delivered! Thank you for the wonderful job you did in designing the CUTE logo. Your patience with me was greatly appreciated as we went through nine versions before we finally got it just right. Thank you also for helping to design my business cards, banner and other materials.

I owe a special debt of gratitude to my editor, Miriam Glover. I knew the Lord led me to the right person because of your enthusiasm and excitement around the message of CUTE. Thank you for your insights, feedback, suggestions and careful work in preparing this manuscript. Thank you for helping me to express my thoughts better. You gave the manuscript the "cute" touch it needed.

And finally, for all my sisters who read this: Thank you for choosing this book. I am truly honored. I hope that you will be encouraged and come to the realization that you are truly a special gift from the Lord, and you can rest on His Word that you are definitely CUTE and **C**overed **U**ntil **T**he **E**nd!

CUTE is written for you, my sister!

You may have noticed that this book is a little different from other books you may have read. First, this is a short book intended to capture your heart and challenge your thinking. Originally, I wanted to write a 5-page pamphlet explaining the concept and meaning of *CUTE - Covered Until the End*. However, I was encouraged by a dear sister to write down all my thoughts, so I did.

CUTE will take you less than two hours to read, but do not take its length to be a measure of its importance.

I could have written pages and pages, reams in fact, simply because I am a talker. Not only that, but I am a fast talker to boot. Whenever my husband would tell me that I talked too fast, I simply said that he listened too slowly. I remember times in my life when I used to think that God was listening too slowly to my needs. In reality, I could not hear Him speak because I was still talking! Therefore, I had to learn James 1:19:

"*...but let everyone be* ***quick to hear, slow to speak*** *and slow to anger.*"
(Emphasis added)

Well, this time I listened to what God wanted me to write instead of what I wanted to write. I am a creative person and I love a good drama, especially stage plays. For example, when asked to write or direct a production, I love to go as far as my imagination will take me. Not to worry, though, you won't find a lot of drama here - just the simple truth that He placed in my heart to share with you.

Secondly, you will not find any hard to understand theological terminology. I am simply talking with you, sister to sister, about who we are through God's eyes and based on God's Word. As you begin to read, you will notice that the book centers around one verse, Psalm 139:14:

"I will give thanks to Thee, for I am fearfully and wonderfully made; Wonderful are Thy works, and my soul knows it very well."

I hope that you will come to a deeper understanding of this verse, just as I did, as you meditate on and walk in its truths.

Finally, *CUTE* is an answer to an increasing demand by women of every age who have been searching for a sense of worth. This book will explain the meaning and concept of *CUTE* and how it is different from the normal use of the word. Knowing this difference will free the minds of women, so that they can live like the masterpieces that they are and become encouragers to others.

CUTE is also a means to evangelize. It enables women to easily share the gospel of Jesus Christ by explaining the meaning behind the name and asking individuals if they are covered. This would then lead into a conversation about how to become CUTE through the saving grace of our Lord and Savior, Jesus Christ. There are many ways to explain the gift of salvation. The model I am using is based on the one taught at my church, Oak Cliff Bible Fellowship in Dallas, TX.

At its core, *CUTE* provides the Christian community with an encouraging, educational, and fun atmosphere for evangelizing to young ladies and women.

There is one thing that I would like to ask each sister to do before reading any further. Find a picture of yourself, you know, where you are looking fun and sassy, and tape it to the inside book cover. Every time you open this book, you will be reminded of how CUTE you really are – on the inside and the outside.

If you are struggling with your identity, the knowledge of who you really are and your purpose in life, I would suggest you read *Spiritual Identity Theft and God's Plan for Transformation by* Carole Whitfield Shannon. She will take you on a wonderful journey of finding and reclaiming your true identity.

CUTE is written for you, my sister. It is based on a simple verse with profound truths. Read it once or read it as often as you need in order to fully embrace these life-changing principles. I hope that you find this book educational, amusing and entertaining. My prayer is that you will discover the wonderful creation that you are and live life as it was meant to be…to the fullest.

Finally, this book is brief because…let's face it, we have been to numerous conferences, read volumes of lengthy books and still struggle with our "cute-ness". We do not need more books or conferences to understand God's Word; it is now a simple matter of receiving and believing it. God said it and no discussion is needed. Amen!

CUTE

My sister, I have just one question to ask, "Are you CUTE?" Well, if you have accepted God's free gift of salvation through His Son, Jesus Christ, then:

Yes, you are CUTE! You are **C**overed **U**ntil **T**he **E**nd!

More to come on this truth in a moment. The point to remember right now is that no matter how the world defines it, you are *CUTE* simply because God said so in His Holy Word.

Psalm 139:14 states:

> *"I will give thanks to Thee, for I am fearfully and wonderfully made; Wonderful are Thy works, and my soul knows it very well."*

Did you get that? Don't read it too fast or you might miss just how CUTE you are! In fact, let's break it down so there is no confusion.

“I will give thanks to Thee...”

Exactly to whom are you giving thanks? Too many sisters are giving thanks to the world for artificial “cuteness”. The world tells us that we must have certain physical attributes to be considered beautiful, accepted, loved or successful. To make it even worse, if we do not fit this definition of “cute”, we are led to believe that we no longer have any worth.

Are you aware that the typical American woman is not a size 2? In an article cited in *American Demographics*, July 1, 2003, the average American woman wears a dress size of 11-14. In our culture, if you are a size 0-6 (you read that correctly, a size 0!) with long hair, light skin tone, blue eyes, and all the right body proportions, you are treated like a Hollywood starlet. You are considered a beauty and are destined to be happy and successful. We are told so many lies, yet time and time again, we believe them.

In an effort to fit this Hollywood image, sisters spend countless hours and dollars searching for all kinds of lotions, gels, sprays, make-up, etc. trying to mold and make themselves into versions of "packaged" cuteness.

I attended a wedding of a friend where one of the guests dressed like a stripper. Not only were her clothes too tight for her large body frame, but they did not appropriately cover her body parts. She flaunted herself and became a negative attraction. It was an embarrassing situation.

Many sisters with large body frames are very beautiful. Sadly, it is often hard to see their beauty because of the tight fitting, cleavage baring and booty revealing clothes that cheapens them.

Even worse, in my opinion, are the sisters who have small body frames with very nice figures, yet try to squeeze into an even smaller dress size. They are so caught up in the world's standards of beauty that they end up looking like women of the "night" rather than the women of "light" that God has made them.

Will they get stares? Will they be the center of conversation? Will they fit in? You had better believe it. They will be noticed and they will fit in, no doubt about it. However, the real question is: what will the Lord say when He sees His daughters dressed like this? How will God measure them against His image of a Godly woman?

If you were to conduct a worldwide survey, I suspect only a small percent of women would describe themselves as pretty. Hmmm, I wonder, if

I were to ask you right now to select, on a scale of 1 to 10 (1 is not attractive at all and 10 is out-the-box gorgeous), how would you rate yourself? Think about it. What is your honest response? Circle the appropriate number on the scale.

I am not too happy with me!		I am somewhat attractive!		I am drop-dead gorgeous!!
1	3	5	7	10

Well, if you ask me that question, my rating would definitely be a 10! Not because of what you or anybody else thinks of my outward appearance, but simply because God says I am!

Most women I have met are uncomfortable with calling themselves beautiful, simply because they buy into the culture's definition of beauty. They focus on the model in the magazine or a particular actress and can't measure up to these false standards. They forget that the life of a model is short-lived. Once the aging process starts or a few pounds are added, the career is usually over. The world tosses the model out. God never tosses you out. He promises to cover you until the end of time.

How many of you have had a glamour photo taken? I had a glamour shot taken several years ago and I remember a lot of fluffing, brushing, lighting and in general, fussing. To be honest, I have chosen never to do it again. Why? Did I not like the pictures? No, the pictures were very stunning. The problem was the pictures were not the real me. They were designed to make me look like a model or an actress, conforming me to meet an image of beauty that I did not create or define.

If I had to describe myself based on a Hollywood figure, I would be more like *Miss Congeniality*, **before** the make-over. Like the actress in the movie, I am very comfortable in shorts, blue jeans, sweats, and tennis shoes, with my hair slapped in a pony-tail. For me, dressing up in a fancy gown, high heels and accessories is torture. Trying to fit the image of a magazine beauty queen, especially on a daily basis, is unrealistic. I may not be the movie star type, but I am still wonderfully made based on God's standards and His Word.

Our young girls look at female idols to determine what beauty looks like and to confirm they, too, are beautiful. They feel compelled to be flawless, not realizing that hairdressers and makeup artists, using airbrushing, lights and other tools of the trade help make these women look perfect. In the real world, women do not walk with an army of "beautifiers" everywhere they travel. However, these artificial beauties shape the self-esteem of our young daughters, nieces and sisters.

Think about the impact these images have on the self-esteem of our young women! Our young girls develop negative thoughts about themselves when they do not measure up to the image of these idols. Without proper guidance and truth, they start to make unrealistic comparisons. Mix in social and peer pressure and media influence and you end up with girls who are confused, desiring disproportionate body figures.

It is no wonder that we live in a society where teen suicide is increasing. Based on the latest findings by the Centers for Disease Control and Prevention, the suicide rate among preteen and young teen girls increased significantly during 1990-2004. The biggest percentage increase, (76%) was in suicide rates among young girls aged 10-14 years. Suicide rates among females aged 15-19 rose 32%. If the comparisons continue to dominate, our young ladies, like some of us mature women, will carry these unrealistic goals into adulthood.

I remember a time in high school when I was determined to become more ethnic. I was fed up of being told I was too light, had the wrong kind of hair, wrong facial features, and…well, you get the picture. I wanted to fit in and look beautiful. My copy of *Jet* magazine determined my idea of beauty and drove me to do some very ridiculous things.

The year was 1971 and the hottest hair trend was the afro! Yeah, go ahead and admit it, you know what I'm talking about! Back then, it seemed like any and everyone who was cool was wearing the afro. Well, I wanted to be hip and cool and fit in, so I wanted an afro too.

Due to the texture of my hair, this was not going to happen. My hair was too fine, long and straight. My mom tried to talk sense to me, but I was tenacious about wearing that "fro"! Trying to get my hair to work "right", I went to the corner store after school and spent my entire allowance on gel products (remember "Dippity Do"?), hair sprays, and other hair concoctions. I spent the next 8 hours in the bathroom applying these products to my hair, in a vain attempt to get the perfect afro.

My mom stood in the hallway, with her hands on her hips, humming a song, and shaking her head. She knew something I didn't. She understood that the only way to get this afro notion out of my head (no pun intended) was to let me see it for myself. Well, needless to say, mom was right!

Side note: This should not have surprised me because my mother is truly a Proverbs 31 woman. As for me, well, I will say my chapter, Proverbs 32, has not been written yet.

I got up the next morning, unraveled all the rollers and sticky goop and proceeded to "pick out" and mold my afro. At first, I was ecstatic! I actually had a big and beautiful afro. I proudly presented my look to my mom and headed out the door to school. She just kissed me and smiled. I can only imagine what she was thinking.

Well, my joy was quickly replaced with angst. I had not finished two classes before disaster set in. "My big beautiful fro was no mo!" I looked like a fool with my hair all over my face. Since I could not go home, I had to stay in school, looking like a complete mess, the entire day. You can imagine my embarrassment. I wanted to crawl in a corner and die! When I got home, my mom did not say a word. She didn't have to because I certainly learned that lesson.

Now don't misunderstand me, there is absolutely nothing wrong with doing what it takes to look your best. Just quit trying to be something you were not designed to be and work with what you have been divinely given.

I can also remember watching my grandmother "do" hair. She was a beautician with a shop in her home. Watching her straighten women's hair was fascinating to me. I remember asking my mom about getting my hair straightened and again she explained why that was neither necessary nor wise.

(Note: Remember when I said I learned the lesson on comparison...maybe I did not really get it.) I was still stuck trying to compare myself to others and be like everyone else. I wanted my hair straightened. Everybody else was doing it and like the way of the afro, I wanted to do it too.

So this time, without my mother's knowledge, (I'm sorry Mama, please forgive me!) when no one was around, I took out the ironing board and iron. I know what you are saying. "Oh, no you didn't." To which I sadly respond, "Oh, Yes, I did!"

There I was with my head down and my face turned to the ironing board. I did a practice run in my head of how I was going to proceed. Confident in what I was about to do, I plugged the electric cord in the socket. I waited for the iron to heat. I could see the white cord dangling across my cheek and puffs of steam wetting my forehead. With one hand I held the hot iron, with the other hand I held my hair and I proceeded to iron. To this day, I can not believe I did that to myself. This was not only a foolish thing to do, but it was also dangerous. I could have burned my hair, my entire head, or even scorched my face.

I am not proud of this moment, and by now, you realize that I have hair drama. Well, you are right, and that is why I won't style my hair much today.

I realize that this story may be a little extreme, but it illustrates the desperate steps we take when we try to be something other than what God intended. It is a self-defeating cycle to constantly compare ourselves to others. To be honest, I had been trapped in both nets: I was comparing myself to how "everyone else" wore their hair **and** after realizing I didn't look the same, I tried to "fix" my hair so it would, even though my hair was not created the same.

I have found the comparison trap to be very draining. Plus, it says that God did not know what He was doing when He made us. We can go to extremes making over every inch of our bodies, all in the name of trying to be beautiful. Then what happens when we bump into someone on the street, at church, or anywhere who in our eyes is the epitome of beauty? We feel defeated. That is why the only comparison we need to make is the comparison to God's Son. How do we compare to Jesus? We were created in His image and He is beautiful beyond description!

Now do not get me wrong. During those early teen years, I did struggle with trying to fit in. **I** did not have a problem with my design, that is, my ethnicity, skin tone, hair texture, and facial features. My dad addressed the issue of my identity early in my childhood. However, it seemed like many **other people** had problems with my genetic makeup.

In some ways, confronting this issue so early in my life may have made me a stronger person. Let me explain.

My family and close girlfriends have described me as strong-willed, perhaps even stubborn, and definitely tenacious. I admit it. I am a fighter. I will not give up easily.

I am not sure when I first noticed these tendencies, but I guess it is easy to develop a fighting mentality when you are teased a lot. Because of my "look" I was called various names while growing up, like "high yellow", "little red", "half-breed", "mixed-breed", etc. There were other names hurled at me that were more descriptive and crueler. Sometimes kids threw rocks at my sisters and me because we were different. Instead of ignoring it, I threw rocks right back at them. My dad decided to nip this fighting thing in the bud before I really did some damage.

After one particularly hurtful day, my dad sat me down and said, "If anyone has a problem with your color, they don't have a problem with you, Pat. They have a problem with God, because He created you just the way He wanted to!" Then he told me to stop being so mean! Huh? Me mean? I never thought of it that way.

I love my dad. He knows how to cut to the chase. From that day on, I never struggled with my identity, race or skin tone again. If you are wondering: "well, what the heck is she?" I am a Child of God who He has chosen to make African American. I am fearfully and wonderfully made, and of course, I am definitely CUTE!

Even though I am an adult, I still face the stares, the questioning looks, and sometimes, the derogatory names. It is all good, because I know who I am. Not long ago, I acquired a new name, "swirl." Now the person who gave me that name can pretty much get away with anything. Sylvia is one of my closest and dearest friends, as well as my accountability partner. Even though her intent was playful, the important point is that this new name has no effect on me!

Like some of you, I had to learn to stop comparing myself to how someone else thought I should look! They did not create me! They are not continually refining me. God created me and He is constantly molding me for His glory.

I must admit that every now and then, the old comparison trap raises its ugly head. Nowadays appearances never trip me anymore. This time, I did find myself comparing my work to someone else's work.

I am the newly appointed "unofficial yet official" director for my church's Christmas and Resurrection extravaganzas. At Oak Cliff Bible Fellowship, my home church in Dallas, we are known for our "spectacular" productions. While directing my first big Christmas production in 2007, I caught myself comparing my work to the previous director's play. Surely, I thought, others were making the same comparisons. To make matters worse, I was assigned this project very close to Christmas and I was traveling for my business virtually every week. The pressure began to take a toll on me.

The comparison trap had me in its grip. Randomly, I would think, "Would this production be as good as in previous years?" "Would my style of directing be as effective?" "Would those working with me now compare my work to this person's work?"

On top of all this, I did not want to disappoint my pastor and those who recommended me as director. The day before the production, I literally panicked and shut down. However, with the help of my brothers and sisters who encouraged and prayed for me, God ministered to my heart. I went to the pastors' preparation room used for Sunday morning services to get myself together before the start of rehearsal. While alone in the room, I poured my fears, insecurities, doubts and concerns out to the Lord, and the Holy Spirit reminded me:

> *Whatever you do, do your work heartily as for the Lord, rather than for men; knowing that from the Lord you will receive the reward of the inheritance. It is the Lord Christ whom you serve...* Colossians 3:23-24

Right then, I gave the production over to Him for His glory. I got up off my knees, and walked out of the room, with my head held high, to start the final rehearsal. Finally, the comparison trap died! I was free to hear the Holy Spirit guide me to produce a unique rendition of "How the Grinch Tried to Steal Christmas!" The Christmas production was a huge success and I was invited to direct the 2008 Resurrection production.

So, my advice to you is to kill all variations of the comparison traps by claiming God's Word. Give thanks to the Lord because He is the one who formed you and shaped you just the way He wanted you. He loved what He has created and He has never made a mistake!

Contrary to what the world promotes as beauty, CUTE tells us that we are **already** beautiful, accepted, successful, loved, cared for, worthy and much more. No matter our size or shape, we are simply all these things because we are *"fearfully and wonderfully made"!*

"...for I am fearfully and wonderfully made"

Let's try this together, turn to your picture that you've placed in the front of this book. Say the above scripture out loud to yourself and keep repeating it until you believe it. In fact, put your name in it: say *"for I, (*your name*), am fearfully and wonderfully made."*

Now, take this a little deeper. "I am" is used as an emphatic statement. Remember when Moses was sent by God to Pharaoh to bring the sons of Israel out of Egypt?

Moses asked the question in Exodus 3:13:

> *Then Moses said to God, "Behold, I am going to the sons of Israel, and I shall say to them, 'The God of your fathers has sent me to you.' Now they may say to me, 'What is His name?' What shall I say to them?"*

God responded in Exodus 3:14:

*And God said to Moses, **"I AM WHO I AM"**; and He said, "Thus you shall say to the sons of Israel, '**I AM** has sent me to you.'"*

God did not give Moses a long, drawn out explanation to describe Himself. He knew who He was and no one else was like Him!

To clarify, I am not suggesting that we should compare ourselves to God. On the other hand, fast forward to John 8:57-58. Jesus is being questioned by the Jews about numerous truths and knowing Abraham.

The Jews therefore said to Him, "You are not yet fifty years old and have You seen Abraham?" But Jesus said to them, "Truly, truly, I say to you, before Abraham was born, I am."

Wait a minute…did you catch that? Jesus said **"I am"!** God said He is ***"I Am"!*** As believers, we understand that there is no contradiction since God the Father and Jesus the Son are one, so Jesus could claim to be **"I am".** Notice, He did it boldly and with no hesitation. It was the Word of God and He was the Word. He was establishing the truth.

My sister, follow me here:

God the Father and Jesus the Son are one and they are both ***"I Am"***.

Galatians 2: 20 states,

"I have been crucified with Christ; and it is
no longer I who live,
but Christ lives in me…"

So, if Christ lives in me, that means ***I Am*** (the Word of God) lives in me and therefore I can emphatically say, ***"I AM"!*** Hence, whatever Jesus says I am, then **I am**! God's Word confirms the truth, so claim the truth!

So what am I? "*I am fearfully and wonderfully made.*" The word **wonderfully** is defined in Webster's dictionary as *"exciting wonder, marvelous, astonishing (a sight to behold); unusually good"*.

You are a sight to behold! Not just good, but **unusually good!** My sister, you can't get any better than that! If there was an eighth wonder of the world, you would be it!

Even if you never hear that you are gorgeous from your father, husband, boyfriend or any one else, it no longer matters. Why?

They didn't create you for their glory! You know that familiar phrase that "beauty is in the eye of the beholder." Well, who is your beholder? The Lord God Almighty, your Creator! He made us and He said it was "good"! You are a thing of beauty in the eyes of Christ who beholds you everyday!

Keep in mind Proverbs 31: 30:

"Charm is deceitful and beauty is vain....."

As the scripture reveals, outward beauty will not last; it has no real value. While we spend all of our time perfecting the outward part, God looks at our inner being…our hearts! The challenge then becomes "how beautiful is your heart, your inner spirit?"

The Holy Spirit feeds the heart of a beautiful woman. Her heart pumps the fruit of the Spirit found in Galatians 5:22: love, joy, peace, patience, kindness, goodness, faithfulness, gentleness, and self-control. Her heart takes God's truth and applies it to life's situations. Her heart is full of praise and thanks to the Lord! The woman that knows the meaning of true beauty will give the same or more meticulous attention to her inner being that she gives to her outer being.

As I said earlier, there is nothing wrong with trying to look your best. Just don't spend your life trying to live up to other people's standards of beauty. God made us and He knows how we really look, no matter how we try to dress things up, change things around, or re-arrange things. Yet He still says we are a sight to behold.

God made you a one-of-a-kind- a masterpiece! Even Michael Angelo could not come close to creating or re-producing you! Think about that for a moment! Say it out loud with conviction. You are a masterpiece. Do not believe me - believe God's Word.

"For we are His ***workmanship****, created in Christ Jesus for good works, which God prepared beforehand, that we should walk in them."*
(Ephesians 2:10; Emphasis added)

God said you are a work of art, His piece of art. Describe the emotion you feel when you gaze on an amazing painting. Think of the high aesthetic satisfaction you get as you marvel at its distinct qualities. You are the work of art created by the Father, your beholder. You give Him great satisfaction! He adores you!

Not only does an exquisite artwork evoke emotions, you begin to see the hand of the artist or creator, his exquisite skill. You are a work created with extraordinary skill by **the** supreme intellectual, your Heavenly Father! You are a masterpiece!!

The Mona Lisa is a piece of art that is widely considered a masterpiece, a unique, one-of-a-kind. It is meticulously cared for, protected and preserved. You are God's masterpiece and He promised to take care of you, provide for all of your needs, and preserve you for His glory and enjoyment. You are so wonderfully made that He promised to **C**over **Y**ou **U**ntil **T**he **E**nd!

Next, look at the word **fearfully.** Usually, it indicates a sense of dread, panic, terror, or an anticipation of danger; however, it can also express profound awe or reverence.

If you were like me, as a child you feared your parents. My father used the belt on the four of us only a few times and only when absolutely necessary. You see, my father's look and the slightest raise of his index finger said it all! My mother, on the other hand, had a way with the tree branches and there was always her magic flying shoe.

Though my parents did administer Godly discipline, I was never terrified of them. My parents were not monsters, and I never anticipated danger for my life (well, maybe sometimes while waiting until Dad got home or while peeling the leaves off the branches for my whipping). Come on, I know you know what I am talking about.

They were Godly parents who lived out their faith and instructed us in the Word of God. I feared them because I had such reverence and awe for them that I did not want to disappoint them. I was afraid of breaking their hearts over something I had said or done. I had and still do have great respect for them. They are a valued part of my life.

We should live our lives in such a manner that people will revere us. Not because of who we are but because of the reflection of our Heavenly Father portrayed throughout our lives. It should be an admiring fear. He regards us as worthy of great honor and does not want any harm to come to us.

Imagine you are in a department store and you are surrounded by very delicate and expensive glassware. Add a child to the picture. As you walk through the aisle of the store, you would grasp the child's hand and gently explain to the child why he or she must not touch. There are valuables everywhere and the owner has paid a high price for them. You would not want the child to mishandle the items and break them.

You are *"fearfully and wonderfully made"*. You are a treasure to be respected and valued. You are not to be touched and mishandled by the men of this world who do not see your value. I am talking about brothers who want to use, confuse, abuse you and then lose you. You are a masterpiece and your owner, Jesus Christ, paid the highest price for you - His life! He does not want His work of art to be mishandled or broken. You are valuable and highly favored!!

I remember boldly repeating verse 14 to my accountability sister. I was upset with my husband over something and I guess I needed to remind myself of this truth. I started reciting the verse and soon I was on a roll. As I started saying, *"for I am fearfully and wonderfully made"*, my friend stopped me and said, "I know you are wonderfully made, it's that fearfully part I am concerned about".

I halted in my tracks and had to re-think just how "fearfully made" I was acting at that moment. My voice and tone projected the terror and danger that was awaiting my husband. Certainly not the "fearfully" God was referring to in the scripture. You and I are exquisite; a marvelous piece of art to be respected, honored and valued. We are CUTE! ***Shouldn't our words, tone and demeanor reflect that truth, even when we are upset?***

“Wonderful are Thy works...”

Some biblical versions read, “**Marvelous** are Thy works”. When I close my eyes and think of marvelous, I think of “majestic, astonishing, and miraculous”. I visualize something so outstanding that it is of the highest kind or quality. Wow, that is what the God of all creation thinks of you! As the saying goes, “You are marvelous, darling, simply marvelous!”

Now take a look at your picture and say, “I am marvelous. I am astonishing, a miraculous gift of God. I am of the highest grade of quality. My worth is of high value. I am something to behold. In fact, I am down right CUTE!”

You can confidently believe all these statements, because you did not think of these on your own. This is what God says about His beloved daughter- you.

God designed you just the way He wanted you to be in order to fulfill His purpose and give Him glory.

In fact, you were not haphazardly thrown together, you were "fashioned". Let me explain.

According to Genesis 2:7:

"Then the Lord God **formed** *man of dust from the ground..."*

Yet, when he created woman, Genesis 2:22 says:

"And the Lord God **fashioned** *into a woman the rib which He had taken from the man..."*
(Emphasis added on both verses)

We know that we were shaped or molded into the image of our Father based on Genesis 1:26:

"Then God said, "Let Us make man in Our image, according to Our likeness..."

Fashioned, however, adds another dimension to the definition. In his book, *Marriage God's Style*, Dr. Tony Evans, Senior Pastor, Oak Cliff Bible Fellowship, explained that the word "fashioned" in Hebrew means "to build". He also stated that God deliberately constructed a woman that man would consider very pleasing. While further researching the word, I found a definition that leapt off the pages of an article written by David Eckman, Ph.D., Senior Lecturer for Kesed Seminars. Found on the Christian Broadcasting Network's website, the article titled, "God Formed the Man and Fashioned the Woman", tells us that the word for the fashioning of the woman is *banah*, used for making forms of art, a temple or palaces. It implies that a woman was designed to be an aesthetic work of art that would have the capacity to sustain her own beauty.

Wow! Knowing we were constructed with great care and value gives us another reason to give thanks to our Creator. Even though His work was good when He formed man, He did something a little bit different with the woman. He "fashioned" her with His imagination and ingenuity! He made her a beautiful piece of art. Look at the different palaces or bodies He created – the variations of our hues, shapes and sizes! Look at all the personalities, skills and talents we possess. What do palaces signify? Royalty!

This reminded me of a comical saying. It goes like this: God made man and said, "It is good, but I can do better, and then He made woman!" Every day and everywhere we go we display His imagination and ingenuity! How cool is that, my sister?

"...and my soul knows it very well."

Remember we stated that we were made in the image of our Father. I think it is important I explain this. I am not saying that God looks like us because God is a spirit. We are "like" God in that He has given us intellect, will and sensibility.

Reflect on the Trinity. God is one in essence (by His very nature), but three persons. He is made up of the Father, the Son, and the Holy Spirit. According to Bible editor Arthur L. Farstad, Th.D., a similar distinction can be made about humans. We are also made up of three components - spirit, soul, and body. If we use his analogy, the spirit would parallel the Holy Spirit, the soul would parallel the Father, and the body would parallel the Son, since this part of the Trinity took on human flesh.

More often, we tend to put the body first and the spirit last. This is evident in the well-known expression "body and soul". Notice, "spirit" is not even included. God's order is just the opposite. God places spirit first, soul next, and the body last. Refer to apostle Paul in 1 Thessalonians 5:23:

> *"Now may the God of peace Himself sanctify you entirely; and may your* ***spirit*** *and* ***soul*** *and* ***body*** *be preserved complete, without blame at the coming of our Lord Jesus Christ."* (Emphasis added)

These distinctions are separate and different and the order is important. The most important component of our being is our **spirit.** In Greek and Hebrew, spirit is translated as wind, blow, and breathe. The connection between spirit and the Holy Spirit starts to become clearer now, as we go back to Genesis 2:7:

> *"Then the Lord God formed man of dust from the ground and* ***breathed*** *into his nostrils the breath of life; and man became a living being."* (Emphasis added)

Why is the spiritual part of our being so important? We are to read and meditate on the Word of God, so we feed our spirits with God's truths. The Holy Spirit's job is to breathe the Word of God to our hearts and minds when we need it and to remind us of God's truths. Keep in mind, the spirit is the part of us that will last for all eternity.

The second component of our being is our **soul**. Remember, our intellect, will and sensibility lives in our soul. The Greek word for soul is *"psyche"* meaning the "inner, immaterial essence of human beings". Our soul is simply our personalities, feelings, and emotions. These complex characteristics distinguish one individual from another. In other words, it is what makes you *"you"!*

God has hard wired each of us with unique personalities. In addition, He has given us the intellect, will and sensibility to look at information and make choices regarding the data. He never forces anything on us. We have the power of choice.

This is important to remember because there will be times when your soul will pull you in the opposite direction of God. When you cry out saying you just don't **feel** like doing what God tells you to do, it hurts too much to do, or it is just not fair! You may even fuss (hopefully, not cuss), yell, scream, or cry. Perhaps you sit quietly, withdraw to your own thoughts, or silently plot your revenge (I know...I've tried it and it is not worth it). Your personality defines you as an individual - even the good, the bad, and the ugly parts. However, there is still no excuse for ignoring God's Word. It is up to us to believe His Word and live according to it.

I experienced this struggle between soul and spirit while writing this book and starting the CUTE ministry. God whispered this ministry into my spirit, but my soul said "Not me, Lord!" The call was too big and the vision included things I knew nothing about. Retail planning, shopping and designing clothes are not my expertise, so how could I run this type of ministry? My emotions were all over the place. I did not feel like starting something so foreign to me. I was content with my work with the drama ministry. Also, I reasoned, I did not think I had the funds or resources to be successful with this new venture.

So what did I do? At first, I ignored God's calling. I convinced myself that it was all in my head and this wasn't really what He wanted me to do. In addition, the economy was in turmoil, people were losing their jobs and homes. The timing of this brand new business did not make sense! Regardless of my arguments, I could not shake the tug on my heart. Eventually, I had to make a decision.

I prayed and asked the Lord to close all the doors in my consulting business and to open doors that He wanted me to go in. I sat quietly and waited for His answer. I think you know the outcome.

Only through trusting and waiting on Him can we make the most of our lives in spite of the world's changing standards. Although we may believe our fears are valid and important, God has not once asked us our opinion. He asked us to trust Him. You might ask, "Trust Him with what?"

> *"Trust in the Lord with all your heart (spirit), And do not lean on your own understanding. (soul).....*(Proverbs 3: 5-6)

In other words, trust in the Lord with the divine truths that the Holy Spirit has put in your heart - His truths that He has breathed into your spirit. Do not base your decisions and actions on what or how you think or feel.

The third and final component of our being is our **body** or the Greek translation *"soma"*. The body is the material part of us - our physical parts and appearance. It corresponds, says Mr. Farstad, to the Son (in the Trinity) since Jesus, the Son of God, took on human flesh.

Today, there is a lot of emphasis placed on keeping the body fit and trim. We have thousands of health food diets and fads, body building gyms, and cosmetic surgeries to improve the body. There is nothing wrong with improving your body and looking good for the right reasons. Will God love you more if you lose ten pounds? No, He loves you just as you are, right now. Do not become consumed by the fitness craze. No matter how fit your body is, when the Lord calls you home, you are going home!

I am an avid jogger. I normally run 4-5 miles at least 5-6 days a week. I run for several reasons. The first reason, and maybe the most important, is I love to eat and I love to eat chocolate! Yes, I admit it. I am a Chocoholic!! For all of my chocoholic sisters out there, it is okay. We no longer have to hide.

Yes, I love chocolate, desserts, and junk food, but I do not like to diet. Just hearing the word diet triggers my body into craving everything that the diet says I should not consume. For me, dieting is not an option.

Also, I am not one of those sisters who eats whatever they want in any amount without gaining a pound. I must burn off that chocolate. In fact, if I see chocolate and breathe, then I automatically gain 5 pounds! I eat chocolate, therefore, I run.

So, I run to stay healthy and control my weight. I also run because it is a time when I can meditate on God's Word and sing praises to Him. I run because I enjoy running. I run because it helps to reduce stress. I run because like Tom Hanks in the movie, Forrest Gump, one day I just started running and I kept running! I am waiting for the day, when like Forrest, I will just stop and say, "I don't want to run anymore!" Until that day, I run.

I know full well that jogging won't stop the inevitable, death. However, neither you nor I should adopt the attitude that we can neglect our bodies. The way you treat your body will determine to some degree your quality of life. Apostle Paul reminded us in 1 Corinthians 6:19 that our bodies are the temple of the Holy Spirit. Give the Spirit your best by maintaining your body. The body is used to carry out God's Word. Your hands, arms, legs, feet, eyes, ears, smiles, indeed every part of your physical existence, can be used for God's glory.

Connecting the three components is the last part of Psalm 139:14:

"...and my soul knows it very well."

What does your soul know very well? That *"I am fearfully and wonderfully made, Wonderful are Thy works"*.

Here's the key to how all this works: God's Word said it and then the Holy Spirit puts it in your spirit! If your "soul knows it very well", then your soul will respond to your spirit. When you believe it, you will accept it and your thoughts and emotions will align with God's Word.

You will **feel** fearfully and wonderfully made. You will **think** fearfully and wonderfully about yourself. Watch and see how your body will respond to your soul. You will start walking like a masterpiece. You will start talking like a masterpiece. You will dance and sing like a masterpiece. In fact, your ears will not accept anything contrary to who you are! Now your spirit, soul and body are connected. Any woman who fully embraces this truth knows that she is truly loved and becomes CUTE!

My sister, God doesn't want you to just know it, He says know it **very well!** Forget about everyone else's standards. God's Word confirms this as a fully established truth.

My daughter-in-law, Danielle, shows us a clear example of this lesson. One day, before marrying my son, Danielle was being gently teased by a young lady in my church's drama group. She wanted to take a picture with Ryan, my son, and asked if this would make Danielle jealous or feel threatened. I stood by quietly and waited for her response. Danielle simply said, "I am secure with my position." Wow! I thought, if she can say that with confidence about a man, how much more confident should we be in our position with Christ. We are secure in God's Word and promises!

Now the only thing left to do is to say the verse like you believe it. Look at your picture or look in the mirror while repeating it. Say it as many times as you need to before closing this book. Say it until it flows freely from your lips. Say it until your father, husband, boyfriend, or anybody else you are close to fully understands that you know who you are in Christ! Say it with gratitude to your Heavenly Father!

Say:

"I will give thanks to Thee, for I am fearfully and wonderfully made; Wonderful are Thy works, and my soul knows it very well."

God said it! Believe it and receive it! Live life as a masterpiece! You are *"fearfully and wonderfully made"* and you will be taken care of by your creator! He has promised that you will be **C**overed **U**ntil **T**he **E**nd and that is why you will always be CUTE!

How to Become CUTE!

"Are you CUTE?" We have learned that if you have accepted God's free gift of salvation through His Son, Jesus Christ, then "Yes, you are CUTE!" You are **C**overed **U**ntil **T**he **E**nd!

What if your answer is "No" and you have not accepted Jesus Christ as your personal Savior?

If you are not ready to surrender control of your life to Jesus, it is my prayer that the Holy Spirit will find another means to touch your heart. However, please do not let the burden of guilt stop you from finding the peace of the Lord. Your mistakes in life can never outweigh His love for you. Give a sigh of relief, my sister; you are a perfect candidate to receive God's grace and mercy.

No matter what anyone tells you, there are no righteous people. Romans 3:10, clearly says:

"There is none righteous, not even one."

Knowing that we are all sinners saved by grace, isn't it time you became CUTE?

The Problem

There is no one who is righteous before a Holy God. We are all sinners. Romans 3:23 states *"for all have sinned and fall short of the glory of God."* We have all missed the mark.

The Predicament

There is nothing a person can do to earn or achieve a right standing before a Holy God. Ephesians 2: 8-9 states, *"For by grace you have been saved through faith; and that not of yourselves, it is the gift of God; not as a result of works, that no one should boast."* No matter how many "good deeds" you do, you cannot buy or earn forgiveness.

The Penalty

Every sin act requires a penalty. Romans 6:23 states: *"For the wages of sin is death..."* The soul will be separated from the body, resulting in physical death. Your body will then return to the grave. Your soul will be eternally separated from God, meaning you will experience spiritual death. Your soul (inner being, that which makes you "you") will spend eternity in hell.

The Provision

The good news is that there is hope. Romans 5:8 states: *"But God demonstrates His own love toward us in that while we were yet sinners, Christ died for us."* God loves us so much that He provided His Son, Jesus Christ, to die on the cross and pay the penalty for our sins. He did for us what we could never do for ourselves! That is why there is nothing you can do to save yourself. Everything has already been done for you. *"For by grace you have been saved through faith; and that not of yourselves, it is the gift of God."* (Ephesians 2:8)

The Process

All you have to do is accept the free gift of eternal life in Jesus Christ. The process is simple. Romans 10:9-10 states: *"that if you confess with your mouth Jesus as Lord, and believe in your heart that God raised Him from the dead,* ***you shall be saved****; for with the heart man believes, resulting in righteousness, and with the mouth he confesses, resulting in salvation."* (Emphasis added). You must turn to Jesus Christ in faith, trusting Him alone and nothing else for your salvation. Notice it did not say you "might", "could", or "there is a good chance" you will be saved. God's Word says you **shall** be saved. It doesn't matter how you feel. Take God at His Word!

Will you now accept God's free gift of salvation and new life through His Son, Jesus Christ? If your answer is now "yes", and I hope that it is, then close your eyes, bow your head and pray to the Father. Tell Him how much you need a Savior, pour out your sins and regrets to your Holy Father. Here is a prayer to use as a guide, but your own words are best.

Dear God,
I know that I am a sinner and I cannot save myself.
I know that the penalty for my sin is physical
and spiritual death.
Because You love me, You sent your Son Jesus to
die on the cross in my place.
Thank you for His death, burial and resurrection.
I accept your free gift of eternal life
through Jesus Christ.
Thank you for saving me.
In Jesus' name,
Amen

If you have accepted God's free gift of eternal life, welcome to the family! You are now clothed in Jesus' righteousness. Learn more about your new life by reading your Bible to become familiar with God's truths. Join a local church or Bible study group that preaches and teaches. Embrace your new life and the new you. From the moment you believed, you became CUTE! **C**overed **U**ntil **T**he **E**nd!

Covered Until The End

Ready for even more good news? Now that you know that you are CUTE, what does it mean to be Covered Until The End? It means exactly what it says. Because you are a masterpiece, created by the Father, He promises to take care of you until He calls you home.

He is the manufacturer of your life and He holds the warranty. So when things break down, when cracks or tears try to rip you apart, when men mishandle you or don't treat you like you are a fine piece of art, when the trials of this world cause you to lose your shine and luster, the manufacturer is there ready to fix the problem. God will cover you. In other words, He has your back!

Here are just a few examples of how you are covered.

- When life hits you hard with a disappointment or hurt and things get so bad that you just want to hit back- don't. Instead, hit the books! Open your Bible and other biblical resources and cling to God's Word. Whatever you are struggling with, whatever you need, He has got you covered.

- When you feel lost with no direction and need guidance, God says:
  "For I know the plans that I have for you, declares the Lord, plans for welfare and not for calamity to give you a future and a hope." Jeremiah 29:11

  I will instruct you and teach you in the way which you should go; I will counsel you with My eye upon you. Psalm 32:8

- When you are lonely or alone, God promises:
  Then you will call, and the Lord will answer; you will cry, and He will say, 'Here I am'. Isaiah 58:9

  ...for He Himself has said, "I will never desert you nor will I ever forsake you." Hebrews 13:5

- When you are tired and in need of comfort, God says in His Word:
  "Come to Me, all who are weary and heavy-laden, and I will give you rest." Matthew 11:28

God is our refuge and strength, a very present help in trouble. Psalm 46:1

- When your enemies come against you, God reassures:
  '*For the Lord your God is the one who goes with you, to fight for you against your enemies, to save you.'* Deuteronomy 20:4

  The Lord is my helper, I will not be afraid, what shall man do to me? Hebrews 13:6

- When you are afraid, God comforts:
  For I am the Lord your God, who upholds your right hand, who says to you, 'Do not fear, I will help you'. Isaiah 41:13

  For God has not given us a spirit of timidity, but of power and love and discipline. 2 Timothy 1:7

- When you lack essentials, like food and clothing, God is your provider:
  He has given food to those who fear Him; He will remember His covenant forever. Psalm 111:5

  Do not be anxious then, saying, 'What shall we eat?' or 'What shall we drink?' or 'With what shall we clothe ourselves?' For all these things the Gentiles eagerly seek; for your heavenly Father knows that you need all these things. Matthew 6: 31-32

- <u>When you struggle with guilt, God offers forgiveness:</u>
  If we confess our sins, he is faithful and righteous to forgive us our sins and to cleanse us from all unrighteousness. 1 John 1:9

  Therefore if any man is in Christ, he is a new creature; the old things passed away; behold, new things have come. 2 Corinthians 5:17

- <u>When you need help in troubled times, God is there:</u>
  Many are the afflictions of the righteous; But the Lord delivers him out of them all. Psalm 34: 19

  "These things I have spoken to you, that in Me you may have peace. In the world you have tribulation, but take courage; I have overcome the world." John 16:33

- <u>When hope is gone, God says trust in me:</u>
  Why are you in despair, O my soul? And why have you become disturbed within me? Hope in God, for I shall yet praise Him, the help of my countenance, and my God. Psalm 42:11

  Blessed be the God and Father of our Lord Jesus Christ, who according to His great mercy has caused us to be born again to a living hope through the resurrection of Jesus Christ from the dead. 1 Peter 1:3

- <u>When you feel unloved, God is love:</u>
  The Lord opens the eyes of the blind; the Lord raises up those who are bowed down; the Lord loves the righteous. Psalm 146:8

  But God, being rich in mercy because of His great love with which He loved us, even when we were dead in our transgressions, made us alive together with Christ (by grace you have been saved), and raised us up with Him, and seated us with Him in the heavenly places, in Christ Jesus, in order that in the ages to come He might show the surpassing riches of His grace in kindness toward us in Christ Jesus. Ephesians 2:4-7

- <u>When you need patience, God says rest in me:</u>
  And let us not lose heart in doing good, for in due time we shall reap if we do not grow weary. Galatians 6:9

  Consider it all joy, my brethren when you encounter various trials, knowing that the testing of your faith produces endurance. And let endurance have its perfect result, that you may be perfect and complete, lacking in nothing. James 1:2-4

- When you need peace, God will give you His:
  Be anxious for nothing, but in everything, by prayer and supplication, with thanksgiving, let your requests be made known to God. And the peace of God, which surpasses all comprehension, shall guard your hearts and your minds in Christ Jesus. Philippians 4: 6-7

  Peace I leave with you; My peace I give to you; not as the world gives do I give to you. Let not your heart be troubled, nor let it be fearful. John 14:27

- When you need protection, God is your shield:
  The name of the Lord is a strong tower; the righteous runs into it, and is safe. Proverbs 18:10

  The Lord is my light and my salvation; whom shall I fear? The Lord is the defense of my life; whom shall I dread? Psalm 27:1

- When faced with sickness, God is the great healer:
  But He was pierced through for our transgressions, He was crushed for our iniquities; the chastening for our well-being fell upon Him and by His scourging, we are healed. Isaiah 53:5

…and He himself bore our sins in His body on the cross, that we might die to sin and live to righteousness; for by His wounds you were healed. 1 Peter 2:24

- When you struggle with anger, bitterness or forgiveness, God can mend broken hearts:
  Let all bitterness and wrath and anger and clamor and slander be put away from you, along with all malice. And be kind to one another, tenderhearted, forgiving each other, just as God in Christ also has forgiven you. Ephesians 4:31-32

  This you know, my beloved brethren. But let everyone be quick to hear, slow to speak and slow to anger; for the anger of man does not achieve the righteousness of God. James 1:19-20

- When you seek wisdom, God promises to give it to you:
  For to a person who is good in His sight He has given wisdom and knowledge and joy…. Ecclesiastes 2: 26

  But if any of you lacks wisdom, let him ask of God, who gives to all men generously and without reproach, and it will be given to him. James 1:5

- When your trust is gone, God says depend on Him:
  Trust in the Lord with all your heart, and do not lean on your own understanding. In all your ways acknowledge Him, and He will make your paths straight. Proverbs 3:5-6

  Trust in the Lord, and do good; dwell in the land and cultivate faithfulness. Delight yourself in the Lord, and He will give you the desires of your heart. Commit your way to the Lord, Trust also in Him and He will do it. Psalm 37:3-5

- When you feel you can't go on, He will renew your strength:
  And He has said to me, "My grace is sufficient for you, for power is perfected in weakness." 2 Corinthians 12:9

  I can do all things through Him who strengthens me. Philippians 4: 13

- When your children go astray or lose their way, God says:
  Train up a child in the way he should go. Even when he is old he will not depart from it. Proverbs 22:6

  For our struggle is not against flesh and blood, but against the rulers, against the powers, against the world forces of this dark-

ness, against the spiritual forces of wickedness in the heavenly places. Therefore, take up the full armor of God that you may be able to resist in the evil day, and having done everything to stand firm. Ephesians 6: 12-13

- When the dreaded "S-word", Submission, is a struggle in your marriage or you are struggling with the lack of a husband, God says:
  In the same way, you wives, be submissive to your own husbands so that even if any of them are disobedient to the word, they may be won without a word by the behavior of their wives, as they observe your chaste and respectful behavior. And let not your adornment be merely external-braiding the hair, and wearing gold jewelry, or putting on dresses; but let it be the hidden person of the heart, with the imperishable quality of a gentle and quiet spirit, which is precious in the sight of God. 1 Peter 3:1-4

  For your husband is your Maker, whose name is the Lord of hosts: and your Redeemer is the Holy One of Israel, who is called the God of all the earth. Isaiah 54:5

Whether you are single, married, divorced or widowed, you have been given a promise by the Father for your provision and protection. If there is a good man in your life, give thanks to the Lord. No matter how good a man he is or tries to be, he cannot solve most of your problems. For some sisters, he **is** the cause of most of your problems. But that's another book, for someone else to write!

We, as women, expect our men to meet certain needs in our lives that only God can fulfill. I know, I have been guilty of holding my husband to this standard. The truth is as much as my husband loves me, he cannot meet my emotional needs. For example, sometimes I cry when I am sad or hurt, while other times I cry when I am bursting with joy. He doesn't know whether to high-five me or wrap his arms around me to console me. If he makes the wrong move, well…let's just say, it won't be pretty.

My husband simply cannot carry all of my burdens on his shoulders. No man will ever be able to meet all of our needs all the time. Most of the time, it seems that it is a struggle for men to even understand what we need. Can you imagine asking them to answer each need? It's not fair or realistic.

Part of the problem centers around that Mars and Venus thing. In the book, *Men Are From Mars, Women Are From Venus,* the author John Gray, looks at the differences in communication styles, emotional needs and methods of behavior between men and women. The book declares that men and women are as different as beings from other planets. For example, women want to talk about their problems. Most of the time, we just want our mates to listen so we can get it off our chests. On the other hand, men want to offer solutions to the problems, thus creating conflict.

The other part is that "they did not create us, so they cannot totally relate to us".

However, there is One who knows all about our thoughts and behaviors because He created us and can relate completely to us. If we have placed our faith in Jesus Christ and focus on His will, He promises to meet all of our needs.

And my God shall supply all your needs according to His riches in glory in Christ Jesus. Philippians 4: 19

There are a myriad of promises to cling to when faced with trials. Go to God's Word for encouragement and strength, because no matter what you are facing, He has you covered! Don't react to situations based on how you feel, act according to God's Word. No matter what you encounter, Romans 8:28 says,

And we **know** *that*
God causes **all things** *to work together* **for good**
to those who love God, to those who are called
according to his purpose. (Emphasis added)

So remember, my sister, if you are CUTE, then He is talking to you! If He says He is going to work it out for your good, then believe Him and...

Rejoice always;
Pray without ceasing;
In everything, give thanks;
for this is God's will for you in Christ Jesus.
1 Thessalonians 5: 6-8

So get your praise on, talk daily with your Heavenly Father, and in every circumstance, give thanks. Notice the verse does not say give thanks **for** everything. Even though God only gives good and perfect gifts, He allows everything (including the good, bad and the ugly) to pass through His hands.

If He has allowed it, then remember, He is going to work it all for your good. So **in everything**, praise Him! Because He is worthy and He loves you so much that He has promised that you would be **C**overed **U**ntil **T**he **E**nd!

The Bible is full of God's promises to you and you can count on His Word being true. There is one particular chapter in the Bible that sheds light on God's comprehensive covering. It is Psalm 23. Through studying the Psalm numerous times and listening to my Pastor explain it in detail, I now realize that Psalm 23 really says it all when it comes to being covered.

Read it for the first time or read it again, with fresh eyes. As you read the verses, you can begin to see how Jesus, our Divine Shepherd covers us. He meets our spiritual needs (verses 1-3), our directional needs (verse 3), our emotional needs (verse 4), our physical needs (verse 5), and our need for fellowship with Him (verse 6) as well as our eternal needs (verse 6).

Psalm 23

[1] The Lord is my shepherd,
I shall not want.
[2] He makes me lie down in green pastures;
He leads me beside quiet waters.
[3] He restores my soul;
He guides me in the paths of righteousness
For His name's sake.
[4] Even though I walk through the valley
of the shadow of death,
I fear no evil; for Thou art with me;
Thy rod and Thy staff, they comfort me;
[5] Thou dost prepare a table before me in
the presence of my enemies;
Thou hast anointed my head with oil;
My cup overflows.
[6] Surely goodness and loving kindness
will follow me
all the days of my life,
And I will dwell
in the house of the Lord
forever.
(Emphasis added)

God is able to meet all of our needs on this earth as well as when we go to live with Him forever. My sister, we are Covered Until The End!

REFLECTION

My baby sister, Debbie, has a 5 year old granddaughter, named Madison. She is a very cute and intelligent little girl, full of fun and smiles.

Every time I visit my family in South Carolina, Madison and I go through the following girls-only ritual:

Me: *Madison, who in this house is cute?*
Madison: *Grandmamma is cute, Aunt Pat is cute, and Madison is cute.*
Me: *Good girl!*

We then high-five each other, hug and do a little dance. We have been doing this for quite some time, although with no spiritual meaning tied to it. Many years earlier, I promised I would tell myself I was cute even if no one else did, so when Madison came along, well, she was easy to teach. Little did I know that God would turn this ritual into a ministry to encourage women.

After about a year of doing this, God planted into my spirit the deeper meaning of CUTE. One day, several members of my youth drama team and their friends dropped by the house for a visit. (Okay, they really came to see my son, Ryan, and to grab some food). They spied our family pictures hanging on the wall and went in closer to check it out. These pictures traced my family, as it has grown through the years. Then someone said, "Mrs. Noble, you were a DIVA!"

Now you would think I took that as a compliment. Wrong! Why? Well, because of one word. You **"were"** a DIVA! I quickly replied, "What do you mean, **"were"**? I may not be as pretty as I was then, but I will always be cute." Of course, they tried their best to back pedal out of that one, but it was too late.

After that conversation, I started to think about the word "cute". It always bothered me to hear the young girls in my youth drama group express their dislike over their looks. We would sometimes talk for hours and I would find myself trying to convince them of their beauty. Of course, they were measuring themselves against worldly standards.

Before I knew it, the meaning behind CUTE was placed in my spirit. Still, I never moved on it. I just started saying it a lot more.

Then one Sunday morning during worship service, God revealed His purpose for this ministry so clearly that I couldn't help but hear Him. One of my sisters in Christ quickly rushed out of service in tears. I knew that her father had recently passed and she was still hurting, so I got up and followed her to the restroom.

When I got there, three other sisters had also come to comfort her. As we talked with her and held her hand, she began to feel better.

As she started to prepare herself to go back into the sanctuary, she looked at me and asked if her mascara was running all over her face. She said she did not want to look like a mess. Without hesitation, I simply said, "You are not a mess, you are CUTE." As she wiped her eyes with a tissue, she replied, "I have never been cute". I then said, "Do you know what CUTE means? It means you are **C**overed **U**ntil **T**he **E**nd!" At that point, all of the women in the restroom stopped and responded, "Hey, I like that…I'm going to remember that!" That was my "Ah-Ha" moment.

After service, I shared this incident with my husband and he encouraged me to pursue the vision. After much prayer, fasting and encouragement, CUTE was birthed into a ministry.

CONCLUSION

I have one question to ask, "Are you CUTE?" Hopefully, you realize that if you have accepted God's free gift of salvation through His Son, Jesus Christ, then Yes, you are CUTE! You are **C**overed **U**ntil **T**he **E**nd!

Regardless of how the world defines it, you are CUTE simply because God's Word says so. I encourage you to memorize, recite and embrace Psalm 139:14:

"I will give thanks to Thee, for I am fearfully and wonderfully made; Wonderful are Thy works, and my soul knows it very well."

Once you fully understand that the Lord deserves the thanks because you are fearfully and wonderfully made, and His works are marvelous, then you can shout *"my soul knows it very well."* Start walking, talking and living like a masterpiece.

You are Jesus' precious child. He is your Divine Shepherd and He will meet your spiritual, directional, emotional, physical, intimacy and eternal needs. Celebrate the unique body the Lord has given you. Then watch yourself soar in your newly found truth!

One day your outward beauty
Will surely fade away
And no one will even give a hoot.
But rest in God's Word
that you are
***Fearfully and wonderfully** made*
And you will forever and always
be **CUTE!**

Covered **U**ntil **T**he **E**nd

We want to hear from you!

To share your personal journey on becoming CUTE,
please contact Pat Noble at:

pnoble@thecutecollection.com
or
pat.noble@verizon.net

For more information or to book a speaking
engagement, please contact
Pat Noble at:

pat.noble@verizon.net

Be sure to visit **www.thecutecollection.com**
for the latest CUTE updates!

Printed in the United States
149544LV00001B/3/P

9 781607 917199